BATAAN AND CORREGIDOR

by

**Wallace B. Black
and
Jean F. Blashfield**

CRESTWOOD HOUSE
New York

Maxwell Macmillan Canada
Toronto

Maxwell Macmillan International
New York Oxford Singapore Sydney

Library of Congress Cataloging-in-Publication Data

Black, Wallace B.
    Bataan and Corregidor / by Wallace B. Black and Jean F. Blashfield. —
1st ed.
        p.   cm. — (World War II 50th anniversary series)
    Includes index.
    Summary: Describes the Japanese invasion of the Philippine Islands and
the defeat of the American forces under Gen. Douglas MacArthur early in
World War II.
    ISBN 0-89686-557-6
    1. World War, 1939–1945 — Campaigns — Philippines — Bataan (Province)
— Juvenile literature. 2. Bataan (Province) — History — Juvenile literature.
3. World War, 1939–1945 — Campaigns — Philippines — Corregidor Island —
Juvenile literature. 4. Corregidor Island (Philippines) — History — Juvenile
literature. [1. World War, 1939–1945 — Campaigns — Philippines.]
I. Blashfield, Jean F. II. Title. III. Series: Black, Wallace B. World War II
50th anniversary series.
D767.4.B57 1991
940.54'25 — dc20

            90-27767
            CIP
            AC

Created and produced by B & B Publishing, Inc.

Picture Credits

Dr. Diosdada M. Yap, Bataan Magazine - *pages 10, 16, 18, 22, 26, 32, 39, 43*
National Archives - pages 3, 5, 6, 9, 11, 12, 14, 17, 20, 24-25, 29, 31, 35, 36, 37, 45
Mrs. Dorothy Still Terrill - page 40
E.B.G. Graphics (maps) - pages 7, 33

**CRESTWOOD
HOUSE**
    Macmillan Publishing Company
    866 Third Avenue
    New York, NY 10022
    Maxwell Macmillan Canada, Inc.
1200 Eglinton Avenue East
Suite 200
Don Mills, Ontario M3C 3N1

Macmillan Publishing Company is part of the Maxwell Communication Group of Companies.

Printed in the United States of America

First Edition

10 9 8 7 6 5 4 3 2 1

General Douglas MacArthur

CONTENTS

Chapter 1

THE PHILIPPINES PREPARES FOR WAR

Pearl Harbor! Hong Kong! Guam! Wake Island! Midway Island! Singapore!

From Pearl Harbor to Singapore on the Malay Peninsula, Japanese military forces attacked without warning. It began at Pearl Harbor, the American naval base in Hawaii. The date was Sunday, December 7, 1941. It was Monday, December 8, at all other targets attacked that day because they lie on the other side of the International Date Line. The Pearl Harbor attack took place at 7:55 A.M. on that terrible, historic morning.

At almost the same moment in time, all of the other targets were bombed or fired upon by attacking Japanese aircraft, naval vessels or invading troops. These attacks were the beginning of the Japanese version of Germany's blitzkrieg — "lightning war." The entire might of Japan's army, navy and air force was let loose against targets throughout the mainland of Asia, the East Indies and the island nations of the Pacific. World War II had come to the Far East.

Later that day, another target for Japan's attacks was about to become a stumbling block to its plans for a speedy conquest. That target was the Philippine Islands, which had been controlled by the United States since the Spanish-American War of 1898.

Located in the Pacific Ocean south of China, this group of islands is called the Philippine Archipelago. It is made up of over 7,000 islands and islets and stretches for about 1,200 miles from north to south. It has 12 larger islands.

Luzon and Mindanao are the largest and most important of these. The capital, Manila, is located on Luzon.

The Japanese wanted to capture and occupy these islands in order to destroy the U.S. military forces stationed there. The U.S. Army and the U.S. Navy were threats to Japan's plans to complete a total takeover of land in the Pacific.

U.S. Army and Navy Alerted

In the Philippines, the attack that was to come later that day was no surprise. At 3:00 A.M. the following message was received: "Air raid on Pearl Harbor! This is no drill!" The U.S. Pacific Fleet in Hawaii was being bombed.

The radio operator notified General Douglas MacArthur, who was commanding general of USAFFE (United States Armed Forces Far East), which included the Philippine armed forces. He also told Admiral T. C. Hart, commander of the U.S. Navy Asiatic Fleet. Both leaders immediately alerted all units under their control.

General MacArthur and his staff gathered at army head-quarters to make plans for the Japanese attack they knew would come. Some watchers reported seeing Japanese planes over the island of Corregidor in Manila Bay. P-40

Battleships at Pearl Harbor in flames after the Japanese attack

fighters took off to intercept them but found nothing. It was a false alarm.

The Army Air Corps Wants to Attack

Before 5:00 A.M. that morning Major General Lewis Brereton, in command of the Army Air Corps in the Philippines, knocked at General MacArthur's door. He wanted to load bombs on his long-range B-17 bombers and attack Japanese bases on Formosa (now called Taiwan). He knew that Japanese air attacks would have to come from that island 500 miles to the north. MacArthur refused to see Brereton.

More Army Air Corps P-40 fighters were ordered to take off from Clark and Nichols fields to search for approaching enemy attackers. In the meantime General Brereton continued to prepare his B-17 aircraft and crews to bomb the Japanese on Formosa. But still no word came from MacArthur's headquarters.

As part of the plans to strengthen the defenses of the Philippines, the Army Air Corps had been receiving new aircraft and crews. It had 35 modern B-17 "Flying Fortress" bombers and over 100 P-40 "Warhawk" fighters. It also had another 150 aircraft, mostly older fighters and bombers. The air corps was ready and anxious to fight the Japanese.

Brereton sent some P-40s and B-17s into the sky to search for the approaching enemy. Finally, as the sun rose that morning, General MacArthur ordered the B-17s to load their bombs and stand by.

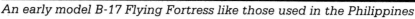

An early model B-17 Flying Fortress like those used in the Philippines

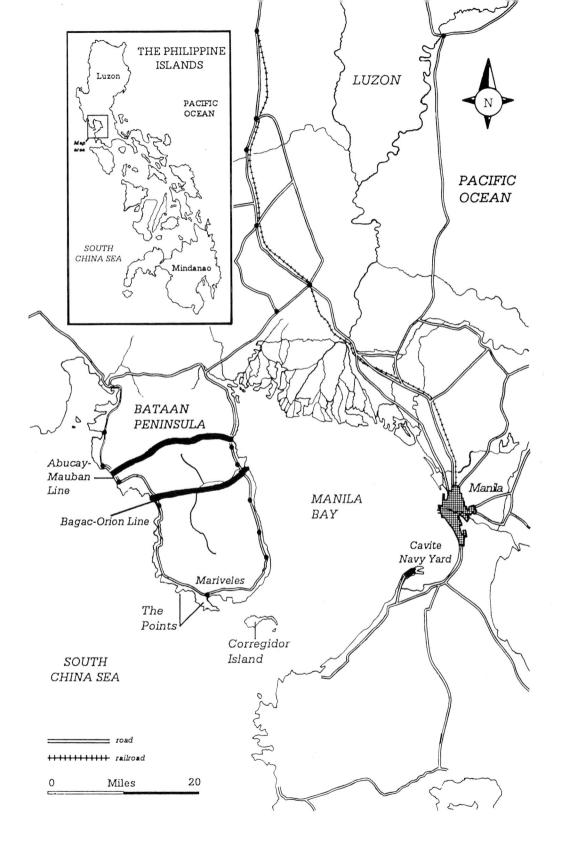

THE PHILIPPINE
ISLANDS

Luzon

PACIFIC
OCEAN

Map
area

SOUTH
CHINA SEA

Mindanao

LUZON

PACIFIC
OCEAN

N

BATAAN
PENINSULA

Abucay-
Mauban
Line

Bagac-Orion Line

MANILA
BAY

Manila

Cavite
Navy Yard

Mariveles

The
Points

Corregidor
Island

SOUTH
CHINA SEA

road

railroad

0   Miles   20

Chapter 2

JAPANESE AIR ATTACKS

The first report of Japanese air attacks on the Philippines came not from the north as expected, but from the south. Japanese dive-bombers and "Zeke" fighters from the Japanese aircraft carrier *Ryujo* drew first blood. At 6:30 A.M. on December 8, they attacked the seaplane tender USS *William B. Preston* and two Catalina PBY patrol planes near the island of Mindanao. Both PBYs were sunk, but the *Preston* escaped without damage.

More than 500 Japanese army bombers and fighters were gathered on the island of Formosa to the north. Just when they were ready to take off to bomb the Philippines, bad weather set in. Several small groups of aircraft managed to get off the ground. Reaching the northern part of Luzon, the pilots attacked a few targets. However, Mac-Arthur's headquarters was never notified of the attacks because the air-raid warning system had failed.

At 8:30, expecting an attack at any minute, the officers in charge of Clark and Nichols Air Corps bases sounded a general alarm. All planes took to the air to intercept attacking Japanese aircraft. None were found. By 11:30 A.M. most U.S. aircraft had returned to their bases. The pilots went to lunch while their planes were refueled.

Out to Lunch

All that long morning there were no confirmed reports of Japanese aircraft—only rumors. At noontime some planes stayed in the air, looking for the enemy. Many others, however, landed at Clark Field, where the pilots ate a leisurely lunch.

Suddenly the roar of diving planes and the blast of exploding bombs filled the air. About 90 Japanese planes bombed and machine-gunned Clark Field. Another large group hit smaller outlying bases. The B-17s and P-40s brought in by the hungry pilots were lined up on the ground like so many sitting ducks.

Without warning the Japanese had struck a crippling blow. Eighteen B-17 Flying Fortresses and several squadrons of P-40 Warhawk fighters were destroyed or seriously damaged. Half of the modern aircraft of the Army Air Corps had been wiped out in one lightning attack.

The Japanese did not get away scot-free, however. A few P-40s that were airborne at the time of the attack shot down seven of the attackers as they were returning to Formosa.

Japanese Mitsubishi bombers preparing to bomb targets in the Philippines

U.S. Army Air Corps P-35 fighter aircraft destroyed by Japanese air attacks

The next day, December 9, bad weather kept the Japanese on Formosa. That gave the battered U.S. Army Air Corps a chance to repair damaged aircraft and get ready for another attack. Only 17 B-17s and about 50 P-40s were still able to fly, along with a handful of outdated P-35 and P-26 fighters.

The following day the Japanese attacked again and again. This time the air-raid warning system worked. P-40 and P-35 fighters scrambled to meet a Japanese force of almost 150 fighters and bombers. Greatly outnumbered, the U.S. pilots were easily defeated.

Flying high above Cavite Navy Yard and Nichols and Nielson Air Corps bases, the Japanese bombed their targets without interference. Cavite was left in flames. Strafing Japanese Zero fighters shot up more planes and buildings at Nichols and Nielson fields. It was another day of complete victory for the Japanese.

But these first days were filled with heroic efforts on the part of both American and Filipino pilots, especially Captain Jesus A. Villamar of the Philippine air corps. He and six other pilots flying slow, outdated P-26 fighters attacked a large formation of bombers, forcing them away from their target. They shot down several Japanese attackers.

Army Air Corps Lieutenant "Buzz" Wagner, flying a P-40 Warhawk over northern Luzon, was attacked by five Japanese Zero fighters. He shot down two Zeros and then strafed Aparri Airport, which had been taken over by the first invasion force.

During that first week of the Pacific war, the Japanese air force did its job well, preparing the Philippines for invasion. The remaining American B-17s were ordered south to Mindanao and Australia. The few P-40s and P-35s that were left would be used only for observation and vital defense missions.

With the Philippines weakened by air attacks, the Japanese could invade the islands without fear of being struck from the sky.

An Army Air Corps P-35 in flight. Older fighter aircraft like this model and the P-26 were no match for the Japanese Zero fighters.

Chapter 3

THE JAPANESE INVASION

Lieutenant General Masaharu Homma, a veteran of the Japanese war in China, commanded the Japanese invasion of the Philippine Islands. He led a force of 43,000 veteran troops, who were protected by massive air support and a large naval force as they charged ashore. All told, the Japanese had over 100,000 men.

Homma had been given 50 days in which to conquer the Philippines. It actually took 150 days. But the invasion got off to a good start.

The bombings left Cavite Navy Yard useless. With the U.S. Pacific Fleet at Pearl Harbor in ruins, no help was available there. Admiral Hart ordered ships of the U.S. Navy Asiatic Fleet that were already at sea to sail to the Dutch East Indies. There they joined the British and Dutch fleets in an effort to slow the Japanese advance in that area.

Japanese bombing raids set Cavite Navy Yard in Manila Bay on fire.

During the first few days, the Japanese air force destroyed or damaged every target it hit. With only a few P-40s and B-17s remaining and no U.S. Navy, Japanese troops landed with little fear of attack.

Even the U.S. Navy submarine squadron of more than 20 subs was unable to carry the fight to the enemy. Because most of the torpedoes stored at Cavite had been destroyed, the subs had only those torpedoes they carried. And many of these were defective. PT (patrol-torpedo) boats and other small craft that survived the bombing were sent to Corregidor or to the Mariveles Navy Base on the Bataan Peninsula. The fortress island of Corregidor at the entrance to Manila Bay had not been bombed.

Landings Begin

The Japanese invasion of the Philippines began quickly. On December 8 a small detachment seized an island north of Luzon. This was to be used for an airstrip so that attacking planes would not have to return all the way to Formosa.

On December 10, 2,000 Japanese landed in northern Luzon. On December 12 another force landed in southern Luzon. The following week another force of 5,000 men landed on Mindanao, the large island to the south.

One American pilot captured the hearts of the American people. Flying a lone B-17, Captain Colin P. Kelly sighted the invasion fleet north of Luzon. Flying through dozens of Japanese fighter aircraft, he made several bombing runs. He scored three direct hits on the battleship *Haruna*. However, his B-17 was hit again and again by enemy fire. The aircraft crashed, and Captain Kelly died, becoming one of the first American heroes of World War II. Americans at home were inspired by his sacrifice.

No major American or Filipino forces were sent into action against the first invasions. General MacArthur watched them carefully, hoping to save his forces to fight the big invasion he knew would follow.

Lieutenant General Masaharu Homma, commander of the Japanese invasion force, inspecting battle damage

On December 22 the main Japanese force finally landed. General Homma and the greater part of his 43,000-man army landed in the Lingayen Gulf 100 miles to the north of the Bataan Peninsula. They had little opposition to their landing. An additional 10,000 troops landed in southeast Luzon two days later. The drive to capture the capital city of Manila was under way.

General MacArthur finally ordered American and Filipino forces into action. They were to drive the invaders back into the sea.

Instead, the Japanese charged ashore and drove inland. General Homma should have concentrated on defeating the weaker defending armies instead of trying to capture Manila. If he had, the battle for the Philippines might have been over in a few days.

Chapter 4

ACTIVATE WAR PLAN ORANGE

In the early years of the 20th century, the United States military recognized Japan as a possible enemy. Plans were made to defend the Philippines in case war ever broke out with Japan. The plan, called War Plan Orange (shortened to WPO), was put into effect in 1924. If attacked by a superior enemy, the combined U.S. and Filipino forces were to withdraw to the Bataan Peninsula and the island of Corregidor. There they were to fight off the enemy until the U.S. Navy brought help.

A final version of the plan, WPO3, was in effect until 1941. This latest plan called for use of air force, tanks and other modern military equipment and tactics.

General MacArthur Takes Command

In 1936 General Douglas MacArthur retired as chief of staff of the United States Army. President Manuel Quezon of the Philippines appointed him a field marshal of the Philippine army. MacArthur planned to develop a force of 400,000 Filipino regular and reserve troops. Regular U.S. Army, Air Corps and Navy units stationed in the islands would train them and provide support. However, the general had little success because there was little money available to build the army at home or abroad.

In 1941 General MacArthur was called back to active duty with the U.S. Army and put in command of all the armed forces in the Far East. Then the War Department started giving him the troops and equipment he had asked for all along. His plans called for an army and air force ready to defend the islands by April 1942.

When the Japanese lightning attack struck, the U.S. and Philippine army units amounted to only 80,000 men. Most of them were stationed at key locations on the island of Luzon. Corregidor, at the entrance to Manila Bay, was ready to fight any efforts by the Japanese to enter this large harbor. It would also serve as the command post if WPO3 went into effect.

Following his return to command in 1941, MacArthur replaced WPO3 with another plan—Rainbow 5. This plan, instead of requiring retreat to Bataan, called for fighting any invasion force as it tried to land. To accomplish this Mac-Arthur divided the islands up into defense commands. Each force was to be ready to fight invaders wherever they might try to come ashore.

Japanese artillery in action against American and Filipino forces

Japanese infantrymen advance in the drive to capture Manila.

The Defenses Fail

When war started on December 8, Rainbow 5 was in effect. Major General Jonathan M. Wainwright commanded the North Luzon Force and Major General George Parker the South Luzon Force. These two forces were to attack the enemy as they landed and defend the capital city of Manila. A third force was supposed to defend the southern islands. Each force was made up primarily of Filipinos and only a few Americans.

When the invasions began on December 10, the Filipino army was not ready. The only real opposition the Japanese met was in the air. A few American B-17s and P-40s attacked the first wave of invaders and sank several ships and damaged others.

On land it was another story. The Japanese soldiers swept aside the few local Filipino troops and occupied key towns and several airfields. Filipino forces fought the invading troops bravely. But the poorly trained and badly

The American and Filipino forces were no match for Japanese tanks.

equipped Filipinos were unable to stand up to the experienced, battle-trained Japanese. Tanks and light artillery that had landed with the infantry crushed any resistance.

General Wainwright soon realized that his small force in the northern provinces could not stop the invaders.

In southern Luzon the story was the same. General Parker counterattacked the invasion force there. But the untrained Filipino forces scattered and ran. Retreating before the advancing Japanese troops, the South Luzon Force withdrew to the north to defend Manila.

Advance from Lingayen Gulf

The main Japanese forces that had landed in the Lingayen Gulf advanced rapidly. By this time General Wainwright's forces were organized and fighting back fiercely. They set up defense lines where their artillery bombarded the enemy as they charged inland from the beaches. American and Filipino troops defeated the enemy in a few pitched battles but soon had to retreat. Led by tanks, the well-trained Japanese troops captured one stronghold after another. The defenders could do little to stop their advance.

By this time General MacArthur knew that his poorly trained and badly equipped Philippine army was no match for the Japanese. And his American troops were too few in number to do the job. With successful landings both to the north and to the south of Manila, the entire Luzon command was about to be trapped.

MacArthur followed his only course of action—WPO3. He sent out the order to all commands: "Put War Plan Orange 3 into effect and withdraw to Bataan."

By December 24 the Japanese had landed its entire invasion force. A giant pincers was closing on Manila and the embattled defenders.

Retreat to Bataan

And so began one of the most heroic military holding actions in history. The 80,000 men of the American and Filipino armies on Luzon retreated toward the Bataan Peninsula. General MacArthur ordered the North Luzon Force to set up several defense lines. Its job was to delay the attacking forces driving south from the Lingayen Gulf, giving all units time to reach Bataan. Outnumbered and outgunned, Wainwright's combined U.S. and Filipino forces fought fiercely and slowed the Japanese advance.

Meanwhile, the South Luzon Force was under heavy attack by more troops that had come ashore on December 24.

General Parker's forces fought back bravely as they retreated northward toward Bataan. A full regiment was cut to pieces on the way. They could not stop the Japanese advance from the southeast.

To make matters worse, Admiral Hart, commander of the Asiatic Fleet, finally left Manila. He informed MacArthur that the navy could be of no help in the Philippines. It had to defend the Dutch East Indies and Australia. And even though the U.S. government promised reinforcements, there was no way help could reach the Philippines in time.

On December 26, MacArthur declared Manila an open city. This meant that all military troops were withdrawn. And, according to international law, the city could not be attacked by enemy forces. This action was taken to save civilian lives and to prevent the destruction of the city. Japanese troops entered the capital city on January 2, 1942.

Japanese tanks entered Manila without opposition.

Chapter 5

THE BATTLE OF BATAAN

Bataan is part of the island of Luzon, across the bay from Manila. The peninsula is about 15 miles wide and 30 miles long. It is covered with mountainous jungles perfect for fighting a defensive action. There were only three usable roads on the peninsula. The island of Corregidor, where MacArthur and his headquarters staff were, lies only two miles off the southern tip of Bataan in Manila Bay.

Over 15,000 battle-weary Americans and 65,000 Filipinos fought their way slowly onto Bataan. Tired, dirty, hungry, with many sick and wounded, they had fought bravely. For three weeks in December and into the first week of January 1942, they were in battle constantly. On January 5 the last troops crossed the Layac Bridge as they moved south onto the peninsula.

This bridge, which crossed a deep rocky canyon, led to the only road onto Bataan. It had to be destroyed to slow the Japanese advance. After the last man and the last tank had crossed over, General Wainwright ordered the bridge destroyed. Demolition charges exploded with a huge roar, and the mighty steel bridge collapsed into the canyon.

The Abucay-Mauban Line

The Bataan force set up a defense line about 10 miles south of the Layac Bridge. It was called the Abucay-Mauban line. General Parker's forces were to defend the east end at the village of Abucay. General Wainwright's men were to defend the west end at the village of Mauban. Mount Natib was in the center of this defense line. At 4,200 feet high it was considered impassable and was left undefended.

Poorly equipped and with limited supplies, the defenders of Bataan made ready to fight the enemy. They dug in all along the line. Barbed wire was strung. Machine-gun nests and tank traps were built. And 75-mm and 105-mm guns were put into position.

The main problem, however, was the poor physical condition of the defenders and a shortage of food. Although bargeloads of food had been brought in from Corregidor and Luzon, there was not nearly as much as WPO3 called for. There was only enough food to last 30 days instead of the six months planned. Everyone went on half rations on January 6.

General Homma thought he was facing a much smaller and weaker foe. He sent his crack troops to the Dutch East Indies. The final assault on Bataan was left to less experi-

A long column of Japanese troops and guns advancing toward Bataan

enced troops. Pursuing the retreating army, they struggled across the Layac canyon. They began their attack on the Abucay-Mauban line on January 10 with an artillery barrage.

Japanese tanks and foot soldiers advanced as soon as the artillery barrage stopped. They had moved only a few hundred yards down the road toward Abucay when they were hit by heavy fire from the defenders. But they attacked again and again, shouting their famous patriotic battle cry *"Banzai!"*

The Filipino-American defenders held off Japanese advances on both ends of the Abucay-Mauban line. But they had not counted on Mount Natib. The Japanese troops slowly but surely scaled the mountain, dragging their heavy equipment with them. Coming down the mountain, they took the defenders by surprise. They drove a wide hole through the Abucay-Mauban line.

General MacArthur, realizing that large bodies of troops could be cut off and captured, ordered a retreat of all forces to the next line of defense.

"Points" and "Pockets"

Just to the north of Mount Samat in the center of Bataan, the next and last line of defense was set up. It was called the Bagac-Orion line. Fighting a greatly weakened Japanese force, the U.S. and Filipino troops were able to hold this line until April 7. Thousands of the original 80,000 men had been killed or wounded. Thousands more were suffering from disease and starvation. Only a small part of this large force was able to fight the enemy.

In early February 1942 Japanese seaborne landings had been made at several points of land on the west coast of Bataan. These attackers were now only five miles from Mariveles on the southern tip of Bataan and ten miles from Corregidor. The Japanese were going to try to capture the naval base at Mariveles. If they succeeded, Bataan would be cut off from Corregidor.

Japanese soldiers using flamethrowers to attack American and Filipino positions on the Abucay-Mauban line

But a small force of landlocked sailors and grounded airmen fought back. Lieutenant John Bulkeley's PT Squadron Three attacked the landing parties, upsetting the planned attack. Other small navy barges bombarded the Japanese as they dug in on the land around the "points."

Trapped in cliffs along the shore, the attacking Japanese force was within range of Corregidor's big guns. Giant 600-pound mortar shells wiped out the entrapped Japanese, ending the battle of the "points."

Other Japanese attacks broke the Bagac-Orion line. Counterattacking Filipino and American forces trapped several "pockets" of Japanese troops. Again and again the exhausted Bataan army fought on to try to wipe out these small groups of suicidal Japanese invaders. The trapped enemy soldiers finally were ordered to return to their own lines after heavy losses.

If the battles of the "points" and "pockets" had been won by the Japanese, Bataan would have fallen to the Japanese sooner than it did.

The Japanese shout into a loudspeaker to urge American and Filipino troops to surrender.

Chapter 6

CORREGIDOR AND BATAAN UNDER SIEGE

The defense of Bataan and the defense of the fortress island of Corregidor were closely tied. Each depended on the other. General MacArthur, as commander of all of the Philippine forces, made his headquarters on Corregidor. The island also provided supplies and other support for Bataan.

The island of Corregidor is the largest of five islands in the narrow channel between the South China Sea and Manila Bay. It was taken over by the United States following the Spanish-American War in 1898. Three of the smaller islands around Corregidor were also fortified.

Corregidor—Defender of Manila Bay

Before the coming of the airplane and aerial warfare, Corregidor was ideally placed to protect Manila Bay and the city of Manila. Through the years a major military base was built. The island's big guns and mortars could fire shells weighing hundreds of pounds over ten miles out to sea or onto targets on Bataan or Cavite.

Batteries of smaller guns were placed to fire toward land or at ships attempting to invade the island. As air power developed, batteries of anti-aircraft guns were also installed. There was also a small air base, Kindley Field.

According to War Plan Orange, Corregidor was to serve as the command post while Bataan served as the stronghold for troops holding off an invading army. Corregidor itself was an even sturdier stronghold. Under Malinta Hill at the eastern edge of the island was Malinta Tunnel. It had been dug through 1,000 yards of solid rock and offered complete protection from artillery or air attack. Command, communications and medical units were located there.

General MacArthur set up the headquarters of USAFFE in Malinta Tunnel. Over 4,000 men and 50 army nurses would live and work in the tunnel during the siege of Corregidor. In addition, there were heavily fortified sunken pits for the big guns. Underground storage rooms housed huge quantities of ammunition, food and supplies. Other troops lived above ground and would find shelter in dug-outs and trenches when the island was attacked.

WPO3 called for no more than a six-month siege. The War Department assumed that within that time the U.S. Navy would have broken through any enemy forces on land or sea and delivered reinforcements and supplies. But no one had reckoned with the mighty Japanese war machine. The 4,800 men regularly stationed on Corregidor were ill-prepared and ill-equipped to withstand the siege of their fortress island.

Corregidor Prepares for Siege

At first, in December 1941, the Japanese air force hardly bothered with Corregidor. Air-raid alarms sounded, but no bombs were dropped. Anti-aircraft crews fired at high-flying bombers and claimed success in shooting some down.

Everyone on Corregidor waited anxiously for the bombing and shelling they knew would come. Defense positions were strengthened. Ammunition and supplies were placed in bombproof shelters.

At the same time, huge quantities of supplies and hundreds of troops were moved from Luzon to Corregidor. Over 25,000 tons of food and other supplies were brought to the island.

General MacArthur and President Manuel Quezon of the Philippines brought their large staffs to the island. Instead of needing food and supplies for 5,000 men as the plan called for, they now needed enough for more than 10,000. On December 24 and 25, 1941, the final movement of supplies and equipment was completed. If the Japanese air force had bombed the island before that, Corregidor could not have lasted more than a few weeks.

Full-Scale Air Raids Begin

On December 29 Corregidor's bomb-free existence was ended. The U.S. Army Air Corps was no longer a threat. Ground forces on Luzon were in full retreat toward Bataan. General Homma thought he could bring about the surrender of Corregidor with a few days of heavy bombing. Then, with Corregidor out of the way, the capture of Bataan would be much easier.

At 12 noon that day, Japanese Mitsubishi bombers attacked. The first waves dropped their bombloads from 18,000 feet. The anti-aircraft gunners replied with deadly fire. Three or four bombers went down in flames, forcing the Japanese to higher altitudes.

A ruined electric power plant on Corregidor after Japanese bombing

At 1:00 P.M. more than 60 Japanese navy bombers swarmed overhead. They dropped their loads of powerful bombs. General Homma thought that these bombing raids would destroy Corregidor just as they had destroyed Cavite Navy Yard and the Army Air Corps bases. Almost 100 tons of bombs were dropped that day. But that was not enough.

Then for five days, wave after wave of Japanese bombers dropped their high explosives. Damage and casualties on the island mounted. Even though protected from bomb blasts, the soldiers' morale suffered as everyone took shelter in the tunnels or other air-raid shelters.

Corregidor had shown it could take heavy punishment. After more than 25 Japanese planes had been shot down, General Homma called off the aerial attacks and turned his attention back to Bataan, where the army was still trapped.

However, General Homma's main air force units had been sent to Burma to fight the American unit called the Flying Tigers. And his ground forces were unable to crack the Filipino-American defenses. Generals Wainwright and Parker held fast to their defense line in the center of Bataan. The forces continued to fight off daily attacks while suffering from hunger and disease.

Dust and Sweat and Rumors

After the bombings stopped, the troops on Corregidor settled down to make repairs. They reinforced all positions and dug more shelters. They continued to help the troops on Bataan in any way they could. Working in heat, dust and with limited supplies, the morale of the troops on both Bataan and Corregidor sank even lower.

But General MacArthur himself had said that help was on the way. But supplies did not come. As time went by food was rationed on both Corregidor and Bataan. Many believed that help would never arrive. Everyone lived in fear of the next enemy air raid or bombardment.

The navy tried to bring in supplies by boats from Cebu

American sailors loaded precious metals and other Philippine valuables into submarines to keep them out of Japanese hands.

City on Mindanao. The plan failed. Submarines from Australia then tried to bring in supplies, but this plan didn't work either. The amount a sub could carry was not enough to help. One sub got through with badly needed ammunition but little else. On its return to Australia, it carried silver and gold from the Philippine treasury.

MacArthur Leaves Corregidor

President Franklin Roosevelt finally decided that General MacArthur should take command of all Allied forces in the Pacific. On February 22, 1942, he ordered the general to leave Corregidor and go to Australia. Although MacArthur didn't want to go, he and his family and some staff members finally left on March 10. As he bid his staff on Corregidor a sad good-bye, the general said, "Keep the flag flying. . . . I am coming back!"

Lt. John Bulkeley's PT Boat Squadron provided four boats for the MacArthur party. Traveling mostly at night, they avoided Japanese navy and air force patrols and reached Mindanao on March 14. From there they flew to Australia.

Japanese gun crews preparing their big guns for the bombardment of Corregidor

The Stalemate on Bataan

Action on Bataan was at a standstill. The Japanese forces were unable to break through the Bagac-Orion line. Artillery fire was exchanged daily, but Japanese attacks were turned back again and again.

On March 15 heavy bombardment against Corregidor began once again. More guns of even larger size were put into action by the Japanese occupying Cavite. Firing huge 240-mm howitzers, the Japanese began to inflict real damage on Corregidor and the other island forts. Although General Wainwright, now in command on Corregidor, feared an attempted landing, none came.

Finally in late March, Japanese reinforcements arrived on Bataan. General Homma decided the time had come to launch a major attack. On March 24, 1942, Japanese bombers and artillery began heavy bombardment of both the Bataan defenders and Corregidor.

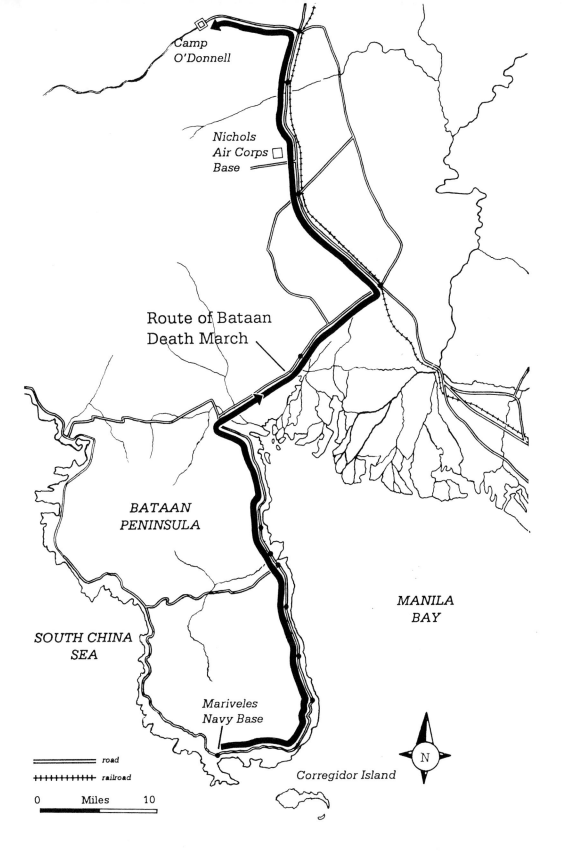

Camp
O'Donnell

Nichols
Air Corps
Base

Route of Bataan
Death March

BATAAN
PENINSULA

MANILA
BAY

SOUTH CHINA
SEA

Mariveles
Navy Base

N

Corregidor Island

—————— road
+++++++++ railroad

0   Miles   10

Chapter 7

THE BATAAN DEATH MARCH

The defenders of Bataan were down to less than one-third normal daily rations. Starvation, disease and injuries weakened the forces.

Finally, on April 3, 1942, reinforced by fresh Japanese troops, the enemy attacked in force once again. Following a heavy artillery and aerial bombardment, they drove a huge hole in the center of the Bagac-Orion line. General Edward King, Jr., now in command of the Bataan forces, ordered counterattacks. But the Japanese forces overran them.

Three days later the Japanese advanced over undefended mountainous terrain. They split the American-Filipino forces in half. The half-starved troops suffered heavy battle casualties. Weakened by disease and continuous combat, they were in full retreat. Officers trying to stop the thousands of retreating soldiers were pushed aside. The will to fight was gone. Escape from the enemy and their continuous fire was the only goal.

General Wainwright, on Corregidor, sent orders for a counterattack. But the defenders could not hold a defense line for even a few hours before being forced to retreat again. On April 8 Wainwright ordered the army nurses who had been caring for the wounded on Bataan to go to Corregidor. About 2,300 others, using small boats and rafts, also made their way across the two-mile stretch of water to the fortress.

By nightfall of that day General King had decided that any attempt to attack would result only in additional loss of life and bring more misery to the beaten troops. Demolition teams put torches to gasoline and ammunition dumps. On Corregidor, the troops observed the huge fireworks-like display and knew that the end for Bataan had come. The long battle was over. It was one of the great defensive battles of history, but the time had come for surrender.

General Wainwright was under orders from General MacArthur to hold out at all costs. Knowing this, General King took it upon himself to surrender Bataan to the Japanese. On the morning of April 9, 1942, he sent a surrender team under a flag of truce to meet the enemy. He signed an unconditional surrender. The American and Filipino troops laid down their arms and became prisoners of war.

Japanese soldiers guarding some of the many American troops who were forced to surrender on Bataan

After it had already happened, General Wainwright received permission to surrender Bataan. From Australia, General MacArthur stated, "The Bataan force went out as it would have wished, fighting to the end its flickering, forlorn hope. No army has done so much with so little, and nothing became it more than its last hour of trial and agony."

The March Begins

Over 70,000 American and Filipino soldiers surrendered on April 9. This was a great surprise to the Japanese. They had estimated the number at about 30,000. Rounding up and controlling these prisoners of war was a difficult task. As a result, Japanese discipline broke down, and the American and Filipino captives were herded like cattle toward prison camps.

On April 11 the misery that would become known as the "death march" started. The Japanese soldiers were impa-

Filled with despair, American prisoners of war awaiting the start of what was to become the Bataan "death march"

Carrying the sick and wounded, American and Filipino soldiers marched slowly toward a prisoner-of-war camp.

tient with having to deal with so many prisoners. They became brutal. Over 300 captured officers and enlisted men in one unit were bound together and slaughtered as a group. Everywhere men were bayoneted, shot or slain with samurai swords by bloodthirsty Japanese soldiers. The sick and wounded were pushed aside and left to die.

Those prisoners who could walk started on the long march toward Camp O'Donnell, about 70 miles to the north. There was almost no food and water. Some Japanese tried to help the sick and wounded, but there was little they could do.

From April 11 until April 20, as the death march continued northward, over 10,000 American and Filipino soldiers died. Through deliberate cruelty and neglect, shortage of supplies and lack of transport, the victims dropped by the wayside.

None of this tragic aftermath to Bataan had been planned. It just happened when all control broke down. The Japanese in command had not been prepared. And Japanese soldiers, accustomed to brutality and war, took out their feelings on the despised and defeated enemy.

The Battle of Bataan ended in a tragedy even greater than the defeat itself.

Chapter 8

CORREGIDOR'S FINAL DAYS

On April 10, following the surrender of Bataan, General Homma turned his full attention to Corregidor. He did not really need to waste his ammunition and troops by attacking the island because the Americans had only enough food to last another few months. But Homma wanted the glory of a great victory. He ordered nonstop bombardment to prepare for a landing on the beaches of Corregidor.

More than 100 Japanese guns, stationed only a few miles from Corregidor, rained shells on the island. The Japanese artillery could fire with great accuracy. Observation planes, and an observation balloon nicknamed "Peeping Tom," helped direct the fire. Everything from 75-mm guns to 240-mm howitzers began a huge barrage on April 12.

At first the American batteries on Corregidor returned Japanese fire shot for shot. Time after time their shells burst directly on Japanese gun emplacements and ammunition dumps. However, most of the American guns, although hidden deep in reinforced positions, were not protected from shells coming straight down. The Japanese soon learned exactly where to place their shells for the most effect.

The artillery duels did not cause many casualties, but on Corregidor they did great damage to equipment and morale. Exploding shells, dust, hunger and the belief that no help would arrive were enough to drive men mad.

The Japanese concentrated their fire on Malinta Hill in the hope that continuous bombardment of the command post would break the defenders' will to fight. But the defenders still fought on.

Some continued to hope that help would arrive. A small force of B-17s and B-25s from Mindanao bombed Japanese shipping and airfields on Luzon. P-40s carried out strafing attacks in support of the bombers. These attacks raised the hopes of the defenders, but the efforts were too little and too late. They were not repeated.

Japanese Air Raids Continue

Although the artillery caused the most damage, the Japanese air force was also busy. On April 29 it conducted its 260th raid on Corregidor. That day was the birthday of Japanese Emperor Hirohito. The Japanese celebrated with a massive aerial and artillery bombardment. Over 100 tons of bombs were dropped, and giant 240-mm howitzers concentrated their fire on Malinta Tunnel and other key targets. By day's end all of Corregidor was hidden in fire and smoke. The hospital in the tunnel was filled with wounded.

That night, avoiding Japanese patrols, two Catalina PBY

Japanese howitzers bombarded Corregidor without stop.

These American army and navy nurses were captured on Bataan and Corregidor. They are shown smiling after being freed from their long imprisonment.

patrol bombers flew in from Mindanao with supplies. Fifty fortunate individuals, including most of the nurses, then flew out to safety. A few more nurses and key officers were to leave by submarine several days later. These were the last to leave the rocky fortress before the end.

Preparations for Invasion

Seeking greater glory, General Homma prepared to invade. He had a landing force of several thousand amphibious troops ready to storm the beaches on the eastern tip of Corregidor and another force to land on the northwest shore.

Landing barges were brought into Manila Bay under cover of darkness. Although a few barges were sunk, enough got through to carry the Japanese landing force.

On Corregidor final plans were made to fight off the invaders. There were about 4,000 marines and other troops in the Beach Defense Command. But few of these men had battle experience or any weapons beyond rifles and machine guns.

With the fall of Bataan, General Wainwright gave his full efforts to the defense of Corregidor. Jonathan M. "Skinny"

Wainwright was a fine career officer. A great soldier in combat, he took over the command of an almost defeated army from General MacArthur. Dedicated to the welfare of his troops, he refused to leave Corregidor when given the opportunity.

As a final act before surrender, he sent Washington a list of all the troops still alive along with their recent promotions. Every man on Corregidor then knew that his family back in the United States would get his full salary during the years of imprisonment that loomed ahead.

Wainwright made final preparations for a last defense. All artillery that could fire on the approaches to the island were manned. With all possible landing points only thinly protected, the few reserves available were placed on alert to reinforce the defenders when and where needed. When they came, the invaders aimed to land on the long, narrow tail at the eastern end of the island.

A Brave Defense

On May 5, 1942, the Japanese assault barges were loaded with trained amphibious troops and light tanks and artillery. The attack was planned for that night. All that day heavy bombardment shook the island. Japanese bombers and fighters would zoom in close to their targets without fear because most anti-aircraft batteries had been knocked out. The defenders took shelter in trenches and holes as they fired back with machine guns and rifles at the strafing aircraft.

The first landings were planned for 11:00 P.M. that night on the narrow strip of land to the east of Malinta Hill. Japanese artillery opened up with a heavy barrage over the heads of the attacking force. When the bombardment stopped, the defenders were able to come out of their holes to check the damage. As they did, lookouts spotted moving shapes approaching the beach. Shouting the alarm, they opened fire.

Searchlights were turned on, lighting up the scene. Dozens of assault barges were surging toward the shore. Heavy fire hit and sank one barge after another. Hundreds of the invaders were mowed down as they struggled ashore. Machine-gun fire and hand grenades blasted the Japanese who reached the beach.

Of the 2,000 Japanese assault troops attempting the landing, only about 500 survived. But that was enough to establish a beachhead and make way for light tanks. The defending Americans and Filipinos were forced to withdraw toward Malinta. Without communications, everyone was confused, but they fought back bravely.

A second battalion of Japanese barges followed the first. Met by murderous fire from the remaining defenders, it too suffered heavy casualties. But enough men and equipment reached the shore to reinforce the already advancing survivors of the first assault. Wiping out pockets of defenders, they advanced slowly toward Malinta Tunnel.

During the long night that followed, the defenders attempted to gather the scattered reserves from across the island. Counterattacks and reinforcements were needed all along the tail of the island. Fierce fighting was still going on near Kindley Field and Watertank Hill. Finally, small units advanced to join the defenders. However, without the help of mortars and artillery, they were no match for the tanks and heavily armed Japanese.

Final Surrender

The battle raged on all night and into the morning of May 6. In Malinta Tunnel General Wainwright had spent the night trying to piece together battle reports as they came in. Information was slow in arriving and was incomplete and inaccurate.

All the general knew was that he was faced with an uncontrolled situation. He expected more landings at any

Japanese troops cheering their victory on Corregidor

moment and thought the approaching tank force was larger than it was. Because of lack of communication, he had no idea what forces he had to fight with.

Wainwright knew the havoc that the tanks could create if they reached the tunnel and the thousands of people trapped there. He decided to surrender. He knew that even though they could probably last another day, another night of battle would just bring more death and misery. It was better to get it over during daylight hours. Wainwright wanted to avoid the terror of hand-to-hand fighting with a superior enemy gone mad with victory.

That morning Wainwright had received a message from President Franklin D. Roosevelt. It said:

"The American people ask no finer example of tenacity, resourcefulness, and steadfast courage. The calm determination of your personal leadership in a desperate situation sets a standard of duty for our soldiers throughout the world. . . . You and your devoted followers have become the living symbols of our war aims and the guarantee of victory."

As word of the surrender spread around Corregidor, most of the troops accepted the defeat with sadness and humiliation. Some vented their anger as they began to destroy every weapon or piece of equipment that could be of use to the enemy. Finally, after raising a white flag and making several attempts to surrender, General Wainwright had to sail to Bataan to meet with General Homma.

General Homma demanded unconditional surrender of all American and Filipino troops in the Philippine Islands. At first General Wainwright refused, stating that the troops were not all under his command. General William Sharp, the American commander on Mindanao, also refused to surrender. But General Homma would not listen. Unless Wainwright surrendered all of the Philippines, the captives on Corregidor would be regarded as hostages and not prisoners of war. They could be slaughtered.

General Wainwright (left) *and General Homma* (right) *preparing to sign the final surrender agreement after the fall of Corregidor*

The papers of unconditional surrender of all of the Philippine Islands were finally signed late on May 6. The greatest defeat—and the most heroic defense in American military history—was over.

The way was now open for the Japanese to advance throughout the South Pacific. Those Americans who would survive the Japanese prison camps would endure more than three years in captivity. General MacArthur lived up to his promise that he would return. In early 1945 he led American troops ashore. Then, under his leadership they went on to recapture the Philippine Islands and free the imprisoned Americans.

GLOSSARY

amphibious troops Land, sea and air forces organized to work together during an invasion.

archipelago A large group of islands.

barbed wire A fence made of twisted wire with sharp barbs placed at regular intervals.

barrage Heavy artillery fire placed in front of friendly troops to shield and protect them.

blitzkrieg "Lightning war" in German.

demolition charges Explosives used to destroy a target such as a bridge.

howitzer A large cannon that fires shells in a high arc to hit targets that cannot be reached by low-level fire.

International Date Line An imaginary line at 180° longitude in the middle of the Pacific Ocean. To the east of this line the calendar date is one day earlier than to the west.

mm Millimeter. A metric unit of measurement. There are approximately 25 millimeters to an inch.

mortar shells Explosive shells loaded by hand and fired from a muzzle-loading tube-shaped cannon.

PBY Patrol bomber, an amphibious naval airplane called the Catalina that can take off and land from both land and water.

peninsula A strip of land attached to the mainland and surrounded on three sides by water.

PT boat Patrol-torpedo boat; a small, high-speed motorboat that is equipped with torpedoes and machine guns.

seaplane tender A naval vessel equipped to service seaplanes.

siege The surrounding of an enemy force or city with the intention of capturing it.

Spanish-American War The short war between the United States and Spain in 1898 in which the United States acquired possession of Puerto Rico and the Philippine Islands.

strafe To attack ground targets with machine guns from an aircraft.

torpedo A self-propelled underwater missile that explodes on impact with a target.

unconditional surrender A complete surrender with no restrictions or limitations.

INDEX